If You Were
A Bird

Produced by Daniel Weiss Associates, Inc.
27 West 20 Street, New York, NY 10011.

Copyright © 1989 Daniel Weiss Associates, Inc.,
and Al Jarnow

FIRST FACTS™ is a trademark of Daniel Weiss Associates, Inc.

Published by Silver Press, a division of
Silver Burdett Press, Inc., Simon & Schuster, Inc.
Prentice Hall Bldg., Englewood Cliffs, NJ 07632
For information address: Silver Press.

Library of Congress Cataloging-in-Publication Data

Calder, S.J.
If you were a bird / by S.J. Calder; illustrations by Cornelius Van Wright.
p. cm. — (First facts)
Summary: A robin discusses the habits, habitat, birth,
infancy and flight of birds.
1. Birds—Juvenile literature. [1. Birds.] I. Van Wright,
Cornelius, ill. II. Title. III. Series: Calder, S.J. First facts.
QL676.2.B33 1989   89-6072
598 — dc19   CIP
                                                    AC
ISBN 0-671-68599-6   ISBN 0-671-68595-3 (lib.bdg.)

Printed in the United States of America
10 9 8 7 6 5 4 3

First Facts™

If You Were A Bird

Written by S. J. Calder
Illustrated by Cornelius Van Wright

Silver Press

Look! Look up! Can you see me?
I am a bird.
I have feathers, wings, and a beak
like other birds.
But I am special.

I am a robin.
Adult robins have an orange-red breast.
In spring you can hear me sing my song.
Cheer-up, cheer, cheer, cheer-up.

Have you ever seen a robin's egg?
It is small and pale blue.
When I was still inside my egg,
I lived in a nest.

The nest was made of grass and twigs
and bits of paper and thread—
all held together with mud.
What is your home made of?
Is it brick? Is it wood? Is it stone?

My mother laid four eggs.
She sat on the eggs to keep them warm.

My father flew around and brought back food for her to eat.

Soon I was ready to come out of my egg.
I pecked from the inside
using the sharp point on my beak.
Tap. Tap. Tap. At last my shell broke.

Crack! I was out!
I couldn't *see*.
I was small and weak
and had almost no feathers at all.

Cheep! Cheep!
My brothers and sisters hatched
out of their eggs, too.
We opened our mouths up wide.
Mother and Father fed us food.
We were growing fast.
We were hungry little birds.

Now I am older.
I find my own food.
I use my beak to pick berries and seeds…

and to catch insects and worms.
Worms are easier to find after it rains.
What foods do you like to eat?

When I am sitting up in a tree,
I see you walking and running around.

I can't move very fast on the ground.
Instead I *hop, hop, hop*.
But there's one thing I can do that you can't…

...I can fly!
I push off with my legs
and start flapping my wings.

Then up, up, up I go!
My wings move up and down.
They move in circles, too.

From up in the air, I see treetops and rooftops.
And I see you!
You look like a dot
because you are so far away.

Sit up on someone's shoulders.
Now you know how it feels to be
off the ground looking down.

Birds move in many ways.

Eagles soar and glide on the wind.

Hummingbirds hover over one spot.
Sometimes they even fly backwards.

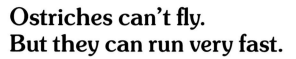

Ostriches can't fly.
But they can run very fast.

Penguins can't fly.
But they can swim very well.

I cannot swim.
But I can take a bath in a puddle.
I flutter my wings.
Splash. Splash. Splash.

Then I preen my feathers.
That means I run my beak through my feathers
to make them smooth and clean.

Birds are the only animals that have feathers. Often the male bird has more colorful feathers than the female.

Robin

Male

Female

Cardinal

Female

Male

Peafowl

Peacock   Peahen

Mallard Duck

Male   Female

As winter comes, food is hard to find.
Most birds fly south.
Geese fly together.

Robins fly in small groups.
Or they fly alone.

After my long trip, I perch on a branch.
I grip the branch with one foot
and tuck the other foot beneath me.
Then I tuck my head under my wing
and sleep.

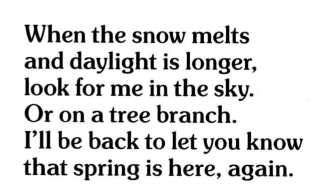

When the snow melts
and daylight is longer,
look for me in the sky.
Or on a tree branch.
I'll be back to let you know
that spring is here, again.